SLOWING THE AGING PROCESS

5 Simple Steps to Look and Feel Younger

Dr. Andrea Eschenbrenner

Author: Andrea Eschenbrenner
Title: Slowing the Aging Process
ISBN: 978-1-77371-315-1
Category: MEDICAL/Chiropractic

Publisher: Black Card Books
Division of Gerry Robert Enterprises Inc.
Suite 214, 5-18 Ringwood Drive
Stouffville, Ontario, Canada, L4A 0N2
International Calling: +1 877 280 8536
www.blackcardbooks.com

Printed in Canada

SLOWING THE AGING PROCESS

Simple Steps to Look and Feel Younger

Dr. Andrea Eschenbrenner

POWERED BY

To your next
Best chapter!
Dr Andrea

For my daughters,

Aurya and Kendra.
You teach me so much.

You are my inspiration.

Learn Resilience

Become Vibrant

Realize Outstanding Outcomes

Expect Wellness

MY MISSION

I create profound life-transformations,

using proactive methods,

so that people can become

active gamechangers in their own lives,

and make on-purpose decisions for their world.

— Dr. Andrea Eschenbrenner

When you've finished this book,
be bold and build yourself a mission statement.
Here is a space, just for you, to state your what,
why, and how.

Writing it in an 'I' voice makes it powerful.

The cover of this book offers 5 simple steps
to looking and feeling younger.
Inner beauty is directly connected to outer beauty.
Less stress = fewer wrinkles,
wholesome food = better skin,
contemplative time = a bigger smile,
regular activity = happy mind and body...
... best remembered this way
MOVE WELL, EAT WELL, THINK WELL,
SLEEP WELL, AGE WELL.

A healthy body and mind makes you shine
from the inside out.
But how do you put it all together to see and feel results?

One little change at a time.

Small changes stick.
From the moment you choose your first small change,
every following change becomes easier.

When you're finished this book, you'll:
Understand more about yourself.
Be eager to plot your journey ahead.

CONTENTS

EXPECT WELLNESS

"The natural healing force within each of us is the greatest force in getting well."
Hippocrates

EVERYONE IS ON A HERO'S JOURNEY

Every person deserves the opportunity to be the hero of their own story.

Regardless of current ability or life-circumstances, we each have something to share with the world.

Imagine what your life would be like if everything—your moods, energy, sleep, intellect, and things you've put down to aging—was functioning, say, 10% better than it is currently.

What if all those areas were boosted to operate 25% better than they do now? A full night's sleep, energy to climb a few flights of stairs, barely a sniffle when those around you are full-on flu, healing faster from injury, defying the norms that come with stages of aging.

Dare to believe being 50% improved? How would that feel?

Does it seem like a fantasy?

I've been part of some amazing transformations in my career—a calling I answered because of an event in my sister's childhood. Now, after more than two decades in the healing arena, I've gathered my experience and created a platform from which every individual can grow.

When you expect wellness, develop resilience, then own your awesomeness, you can celebrate the outcome. I'll lay the groundwork for that.

WHY I WROTE THIS BOOK

This powerful book came about because of my story of perseverance and resilience. The challenges included living in another country with no extended family and, while there, becoming a mother to two daughters while being married to a man who had some challenges of his own. It was difficult finding myself, a professional—he was a professional too—in such a helpless situation. Stress almost got the better of me. The custody struggles before I returned to Canada required monumental strength to handle. I've come a long way.

My wanting to help others heal and reach their potential is served by effecting positive change inside and outside my practice. In the office, I change one person at a time—and that is a wonderful thing. Two decades later—and many changed people—I decided I could share the messages I give to my patients with more people than I could ever see in my practice.

This book takes me out of my office and puts me in the space of many. That said, I'm going to talk to you in this book as if the two of us are together in conversation—hence the word 'you'. I consider it a success if you simply read this book and go on to apply some of the things that are covered here. If you end up joining me for coaching and courses, that's great too.

This book is less than a course and more than a starter conversation. It covers a lot, yet it doesn't dive too deeply into details. No one needs to feel overwhelmed when they begin major life changes. Starting with some basics and proceeding slowly is powerful because it is realistic—it meets us where we are. For that reason, I have chosen, for the most part, not to be specific on dosages of supplements, measurements of food, or duration of exercise; those things are highly individual . I am happy to guide those who contact me for specifics.

Now that I've shared a little of my story, I want you to have the chance to share yours. Yes, YOU share your story. Really.

You might wonder why you would share your story when I won't be able to read it. The thing is, I don't need to: Someone much more relevant than me needs to read your story. YOU.

By sharing your major milestones and downfalls in your life, you will be well positioned to make changes. Having your life so far, right in front of you, in one 'outline', is a vital step to re-establishing your foundation.

We easily forget ourselves. I want YOU to be memorable to you.

To recap: This book allows me to fulfill my mission of helping people become the best decision-makers ever. It allows me to reach a larger group, rather than one at a time. Helping others: that's why I'm writing this book.

Why are you reading this book?

This is as much your book as it is mine. I want YOU to know why you are going to read it, before you start—or at least before you get to the end of this section.

The best way to achieve what the cover offers is first to understand where you are and how you got here, to this book.

Have you ever gone over your personal life story in terms of the highlights, lowlights, and milestones? Many of us tend to focus on one extreme or the other, instead of looking at a balance of both.

EXPECT WELLNESS

- Looking and feeling younger is an inside job.
- Total health creates a glow.
- Significant change comes through small steps.

CALL TO ACTION:

MAKE YOURSELF A PRIORITY: INTERACT WITH THIS BOOK.

THE OUTSTANDING AND BREATHTAKING YOU

When we're busy riding the highs, we don't take the time to analyze why it's going right. When we are entrenched in the lows, we are too preoccupied with frustration or sadness to examine and learn.

We have to know where we are (and how we got here) if we are going somewhere else.

In a sentence or two, on paper or on your phone's notebook or recorder, overview the story of your life by applying a phrase to stages of your life, and hitting some of the key highs and lows.

Fill in these 'I' statements as best as you can.

These are the messages I was given before I was ten: (example: artistic, messy, mean, kind... what roles was I assigned?)

___

___

___

___

In junior high, I recall these milestones in my family, and in my circle of friends.

People I looked up to:

In high school, I believed this about myself:

I'd summarize my life between twenty and thirty as:

Significant events in my thirties:

Past thirty, in five- or ten-year increments, these are some of the wonderful and not so wonderful things that happened:

It is often a relief to have a few words about specific events in life. Thank you for being honest and taking part in this.

A word that describes where you think you are right now? Several words?

Are you being fair with your evaluation? Have you been ashamed to write certain things? You can simply write yes or no in answer to that question, or you could choose a phrase to describe it and get it out of your head.

____

____

____

____

Are you resentful toward anyone? Were you taught to let sleeping dogs lie or not to upset the apple cart? Reminder: No one else ever has to see your answer.

____

____

____

Helpful words to use if you've left some blanks, and were not sure what to use. Confused stuck spiralling (downwards) happy successful loving disrupted mean unhealthy suspicious dishonest sad depressed elated accomplished kind giving connected intelligent enthusiastic energetic clear-minded driven jealous dysfunctional addicted abusive trapped free oppressed bossy shy peaceful confrontational unproductive unfinished unworthy used unwanted worthy helpful overwhelmed unfocussed driven.

Some words on the list may trigger negative feelings. Please do the best you can to be aware of the impact the word has on you, then pass it by. Remind yourself this may be the most honest you've been with yourself in a long time. Be proud of your courage to be aware, answer, and adventure into new territory.

Even though you don't need to analyze your notes at this moment, you are closer to knowing where you've been and where you are now. This is the perfect place from which to move on.

Let's start with some positives. No evaluating needed. Think with your heart not your head. Write down three things that you love about yourself:

1 ______________ 2) ______________ 3) ______________

When you've done that, here's a challenge. Given all you have overviewed about your life to see what got you here, try this: Fifteen more positives throughout your life, about you, in any way shape or form.

There are fifteen spaces here.

Struggling? Fifteen can be hard for someone who is hard on themself. It's necessary to see those words in order to take on self-growth, and to carry you through change and power your resilience development. Some of those positives are directly related to your resilience and you just didn't realize it.

Here's an example:

Smile at people	Volunteered at foodbank	Pick up trash when I see it in street	Received award in school for kindness	Remember birthdays
Punctual	Follow through on what I say I'll do	Consider other people's feelings	Have nice handwriting	Turned in a wallet I found
Paid for someone's coffee order in the drive thru	Sometimes put friendly notes in children's lunches	Walked away from drama with my sister	Gave myself permission to take a break	I am a good listener

It can feel awkward to own your 'own' awesomeness. How do you think you'd feel with 30 phrases? Would you feel positively braggy if you filled out a grid of 100? Here's an idea: Next time you are with a few friends, grab some paper and create grids for all of you; challenge yourself again, and them.

These positives will allow you to see qualities are already in your toolbox.

EXPECT WELLNESS

- The best way to get somewhere is to know where you've been.
- The best way to get somewhere is to know where you are.
- Take the time to get to know you; you are worth knowing.

THE WEEKEND CONFERENCE EFFECT

What is a healthy lifestyle? How meaningful will your life be? How long will you live?

There is a paradox many of us face, especially those of us over forty, which is, when we hear of a friend's illness and diagnosis, we are immediately moved. If the outlook is terminal, we are devasted for them. Yet, within all this we are also relieved—we might not like to admit it, but we feel fortunate it is not us. Certainly, in situations where the person is our child, we would trade places in a heartbeat but, when it is a more distant, we are secretly grateful it is not us. In these situations, we offer help, deliver meals, or run our friend's children to school but, when we're on our own, the words 'it could have been me' come to mind. It is then that we find ourselves vowing to change our habits.

For a while, we consider our own mortality. We might even lose ten pounds or start walking, or reduce stress by not working so much overtime. But, usually, within a short time, we go back to what we were doing before. Creatures of habit, our practices are ingrained within us with a kind of permanent marker that is almost impossible to remove. We only make change when we are desperate—and not always then.

We are a society that looks for cures once we get a disease, rather than one which actively prevents it.

Preventing disease means sacrifice and hard work—that's what we tell ourselves. But that is a flawed perception. While some may feel what constitutes creating a healthy lifestyle is daunting, it is only overwhelming when we throw every 'must do' at ourselves all at once.

The secret to complete lifestyle change is to find someone who can provide solid, basic information on wellness, learn from them, then incorporate their advice a little at a time until those things become a regular practice. For example: drinking half a glass of water in the morning becomes a full glass. One flight of stairs at work becomes two. Two nights a week without a device in your bedroom becomes four.

The opposite of small change is the all-in right-now action. For example, the two-day seminar, touted as a life-changer, may be an amazing event but, if we have not already come to terms with where we are and what is needed when we sign up for such an event, well, the two day event is just that: a two day 'fast track' to all the changes we want to see.

SCENARIO ONE

Cheryl is someone we all know. She is kind and fun and she tries hard to make a difference in the lives of others and, sometimes, forgets about her own. She can also be a bit impulsive sometimes, especially when it has to do with solutions—for example, she's been all over that lose 30 in 30 a few times.

Recently, Cheryl's friend tagged her in a Facebook offer for a two day change your life event. The images of the mountains in the meme bring about a peaceful feeling in Cheryl, and those before and after pictures of women who attended last year's event, and have turned around their lives, convince her to sign up. Hours later she has printed off the input forms, sent along with the $1000.00 investment in herself.

On the day Cheryl is to drive to the event in a nearby mountain town, she feels a little deflated. She's not done the self analysis or prerequisite reading. With half an hour to go before leaving the house, she curses herself, remembering how she was going to have the house clean so that, when she got back from the event, she'd be walking into a new life.

She rushes the kids to the car and, before she's a block away, wonders if she unplugged the iron that was supposed to be used to press the shirt she planned to wear to the meet and greet. Her suitcase contains the wrinkled shirt and a stretchy sweater as a go-to if she can't iron it in her room.

Guilt overwhelms her at her parents' home—she hasn't visited them for ages. The drop off requires a little chat, putting Cheryl further behind. Later, as she speeds down the highway, she avoids a ticket—someone has already been pulled over.

The good thing about being late is that there is no line up at the check in. But it does not allow time to fill in the self analysis—and what about that reading? Cheryl barely notices the mountain view as she unsuccessfully searches for an iron. "This is a conference to change my life?"

At the end of two days, Cheryl's envelope is filled with pamphlets. She's met lovely people, and is filled with inspiration. The only thing is, Cheryl's heart is telling her she wasn't prepared, and that she's not really ready to dive into all this.

The conference swag includes checklists to be filled in every day. The exercise poster features a toned woman in her twenties who has likely never juggled two children and a full-time job, all while living in a house with a leaky roof.

The kids bounce to the car, full of junk food. Cheryl is hungry too and, though she'd been invited by a group of women to stay late and have a meal at the lodge in the mountains, she knew that her parents were expecting her—this is their bridge night.

Immediately, Cheryl gets the kids to the table for homework since none was done at their grandparents'. She demands they stay put while she tapes up the poster of nutritious snack ideas. Brother and sister argue. Cheryl's stomach growls. She orders pizza.

When the kids are in bed, the app she downloaded at the event chimes to remind it is time for meditation—. But, holy crap, it's half an hour long and Cheryl doesn't even have fifteen minutes because her work clothes aren't ready plus she's got a bit of reading to do before a meeting tomorrow and there's laundry in the washer that needs putting in the dryer. *Whew.*

Wellness events are great, and they can inspire, but the habits of a lifetime cannot be transformed over a two-day weekend.

SCENARIO TWO

Cheryl's friend has sent her an ad on social media for a two-day wellness event. She'd love to go. She checks herself. Sure, she's saved some money to treat herself, but there's a little voice in her head, or her heart, or her gut... the chiropractor she saw last year talked about small changes; Cheryl wishes she'd continued to get checkups, even though her back was better.

Cheryl decides she will not go to the wellness event; she's not ready, and it's the mountains that are calling to her. Instead, the next Saturday, she takes the kids out that way. The fresh air and space are freeing. A few days after, an email arrives from a girlfriend she hasn't seen for ages. A few women are going for a gentle hike not far from where she's just taken the kids—would she like to go?

She gets her parents to babysit for an overnight—her friends insisted they have a nice dinner before returning—and she sleeps in before she gets the kids on Sunday. She has not meditated, she has not changed her diet, but she drank more water because of the exertion on the hike. And she's gone online and scheduled a chiropractor appointment. Nothing feels overwhelming. Cheryl feels great for having gone on the hike. She even has a seed of a daydream: what if I found a job out in a mountain town?

She orders pizza for the kids; eats two pieces and puts two in a container for her work lunch tomorrow. She's just not as hungry as usual. She settles the kids so she can watch an online video about the Glacier at Bow Lake. There's a walk that her friends spoke of.

She changes her screensaver to the mountain shot she took one hour into the hike—three deer at the edge of a lake. Positively serene. When she gets into bed, she closes her eyes and pictures the mountains, then lists a few things she's grateful for.

The next day, Cheryl forgets the pizza in the fridge, so buys a quinoa salad at 11:00, eats it at her desk, then heads to a walking path not far from the office.

One month later, Cheryl's nighttime gratitude lists have extended to include five minutes of journal writing. Four out of five lunchtimes she's walking the trail. Sunday pizzas are now homemade, and the kids participate. Who knew cauliflower crust could be so good? Jamie has stopped having tummy aches—Cheryl connects this to gluten. Every dinnertime she and the kids talk about the best part of their day.

Two months later, the family is gluten free. It's easier for everyone, rather than one family member. The hikes with girlfriends have evolved to organized outings with fifteen women.

A quick step on the scale reveals a four-pound loss since she considered that $1000 event. If she were to sign up for the next one, she knows that she'd be in better mental shape to take in the presentations but, for right now, slow and steady, adding a little at a time, is suiting her just fine.

That few minutes of positive thought at bedtime, so doable. Brushing her teeth in the morning is combined with some side kicks—not keeping count, just moving. That little dance action when she gets out of the shower is becoming quite choreographed. The lunchtime walks, and weekend hikes, are giving her more exercise than ever.

Sleep comes easily and it is deep and restful—it helps that the room is not cluttered, and the electronics are banished from bedtime. Decisions at work are seamless and rarely does she bring any work home. The chiropractor has aligned her and given her a few stretches to do at work. Her groceries are now ordered online from a local company that delivers healthy, organic food. Healthy lunches are now brought to work from home instead of being purchased from a concession.

Slowly... changing...

Six months later, Cheryl finds it hard to recognize herself. She's down ten pounds, but that is nothing compared to her glow. Her smile is brighter. Her energy is off the charts. She now meditates several times a week, and has the kids doing it too.

The friend who sent her the ad—and went to the two-day event—visits. She shares that she has not made any changes at all and is even heavier than when she went. Cheryl tells her: "Don't try to change everything at once."

After her friend has gone, Cheryl walks by the hall mirror and moves in for a closeup.

"I look younger," she says. She skips away. "Hey, I feel younger."

****

There are many amazing wellness events which are well organized. If you want to, sign up. But first, understand your expectations.

We can all take a page from Cheryl's second scenario. When we identify our passion, and move slowly in the direction of wellness, we receive so much. Can't you imagine her finding a job- listing in that mountain town, and living out her dreams?

EXPECT WELLNESS

- There are no quick fixes—small changes done consistently create habits.
- Change is more effective when you listen to your heart and do something you love.
- Be good to yourself and contribute to your own growth.

CALL TO ACTION

USE THIS BOOK AS A SOLID,
BASIC INFORMATION SOURCE.

FOLLOW ME ON FACEBOOK TO ESTABLISH
A RELATIONSHIP, AND TO KEEP THAT
INFORMATION FLOWING.

THE FIRST SIMPLE STEP: MOVE WELL

"Get knowledge of the spine, for this is the requisite for many diseases."
Hippocrates

BACKGROUND

It wouldn't be my book if I didn't include chiropractic.

My sister had her first seizure at 10 months; she was ambulanced to the hospital. The seizures came out of the blue, and the doctor's solution was to put her on Dilantin. A couple of months after taking the meds, she developed a severe skin reaction, swelling, redness, and a high fever. Again, she was returned to the hospital, and my parents were told this poor little child was severely allergic to the medication, so another drug was prescribed. The downside to this new drug was that it could damage her liver. She had monthly check-ups to monitor it.

A few months on this new drug saw her go from a happy, vibrant child who had one seizure, to a non-responsive child who was losing her hair in chunks and didn't answer her name. My parents became desperate to figure out what they could do to help.

My parents were told that there was a lot of epileptic activity in my sister's brain and, without this awful medication, my sister would have more Grand Mal seizures during the night and, eventually, she would become brain dead.

At that time, a friend of my mom's suggested that my sister be taken to the friend's chiropractor. Like most people, my mom thought chiropractic was for back and neck pain; fortunately, she was willing to try it.

The chiropractor examined my sister and took x-rays of her neck to see what could possibly have triggered the seizures. After an extensive evaluation, his final diagnosis was that during the birthing process there was such a force placed on her neck, especially to the top vertebrae in her spine, that there was pressure on her brain stem.

Within six months of chiropractic treatments, her seizures stopped. With no medication, she became just like any other child. Now, obviously, I can't say that chiropractic cures epilepsy, but it certainly helped my sister. She is now a beautiful, healthy mother of three children. She's never had a single reoccurrence of those seizures.

WHAT IS CHIROPRACTIC?

Chiropractic care is a profession which is about making sure the nervous system is fully functional.

Just like you get your teeth checked or you get your eyes checked, you get your nervous system checked. Chiropractors are the only professionals who can do that.

Without the nervous system, a complex network of nerves and cells that carry messages to and from the brain and spinal cord to various parts of the body, we would not function. This powerful little book is not meant to overwhelm you with medical terminology; for now, just think communication—a massive highway that carries vital information through your body to keep you alive.

Just like small, positive changes over time will combine to become a whole wellness lifestyle, small increments of neglect, including ignoring little pains, will accumulate and may become a major problem.

When we get small, recurring discomforts, we can easily let it go. We hardly notice because we are great at putting up with the pain—or covering it up. We find another way to bend to avoid the pain in our side. We buy different shoes that slip on. We avoid getting on the floor to play with the kids. We take pills. All the while, what we are ignoring is compounding. A light headache once a week is written off because of too much screen time; a tingle in the hands, we put down to overwork and aging.

The thing is, those little pains are alarms to let us know that something is amiss. So many Canadians suffer from pain and chronic pain—all day and every day. When it becomes intolerable, the answer is to see a medical doctor who will prescribe medication to alleviate the suffering.

Medications, in general, do not heal the body; they suppress symptoms—take the pain away.

Can you imagine if the check engine light went on in your car and you put a piece of black tape over the display so you didn't see the light? But has the problem gone away? Of course not. With the black tape solution, the car will break down and there will be major repairs to deal with.

When we do not pay attention to the warning, well, you get it.

The pharmaceutical industry capitalizes on a culture of ignoring or not wanting to see warning lights. Drugs are advertised for every problem we have: Amoxicillin for infants, Ritalin for children, appetite suppressants for teenagers, No-Doz or caffeine for young adults, Prozac for young mothers, Zantac for middle-aged adults, a cocktail of sometimes dangerous combinations for the elderly. All drugs have side effects. Not all medication is bad, but medication does not always need be the first line, and only line, accessed to help the body become healthier.

Many people take non-steroidal, anti-inflammatory drugs known as NSAIDs, like Ibuprofen or Naproxen, to decrease pain. It terrifies me that people take it like candy; NSAIDs can increase the risk of heart attack and stroke. That is serious! One common side effect of these drugs is gastrointestinal bleeding from ulcers. My dad was prescribed Naproxen for his Rheumatoid Arthritis. After a time, he was hospitalized with a bleeding ulcer. Just because the pharmacy stocks tablets on its shelves doesn't mean those medicines are harmless; doesn't mean the pills will take care of your issue, either.

Headaches, carpal tunnel syndrome, numbness in arms and hands, shoulder pain, mid back pain, pinched nerve, sciatic pain, knee pain, and plantar fasciitis are all manageable and, in most cases, chiropractic helps.

Twenty years into chiropractic, I wholeheartedly believe:

- The body can self-heal and self-regulate.
- The brain and nervous system controls and coordinates every organ, tissue, and cell.
- Anything that interferes with this communication process can cause the body to malfunction, which can lead to disease and symptoms.

Anything that removes this interference, such as a chiropractic adjustment, can restore the communication between your brain and your body, allowing the body to function optimally and therefore heal itself.

Let's return to the nervous system.

The brain sends messages, through the spinal cord, to the whole body. The spinal cord has nerves that come out at each level of the spine and go to every organ, tissue, and cell in the body.

If you were to touch a hot stove with your hand, the pain signal from your hand is sent to your brain before you even have a chance to register what happened. Then your brain sends a signal to the muscles in your arm so that you will quickly pull your hand away. That's how amazing your nervous system is.

A healthy spine means a healthy body. When a spinal segment doesn't move well, it negatively impacts brain function. The brain then loses the capacity to perceive and respond to all the information it receives from your body. If your brain can accurately perceive what is going on, it can control your body better. Chiropractic adjustments help restore the function of your spine which improves the communication between your brain, body, and environment.

Spinal segments that don't move well are called subluxations/fixations. There are three (main) reasons they occur:

Emotional stress. Every human responds to stress with a fight-or-flight response—this is our sympathetic system. If a bear comes at you, you either get strong enough to fight the bear or strong enough to run like crazy. When the bear is no longer there, any damage that may have happened during the fending off of the bear will get healed with the parasympathetic system.

But, when you encounter emotionally fraught situations: dealing with a nasty divorce, pressure from a difficult employer, financial hardship, shame and regret regarding a family crisis—the fending off is no longer an event where you fight and the enemy leaves; it is like the bear has his arm around your shoulders 24/7. This constant fending off of the emotional-weight causes sleep and digestive issues: in the grand scheme of things, how could you possibly be trying to sleep or eat if you're fighting off a bear? This repetitive emotional stress—the burden—causes muscles to contract, which then leads to muscle spasms, guarding, and compensations in your posture, which lead to spinal fixation.

Physical stress. It is not just the slips, falls, bumps, or incorrect lifting, but the repetitive daily actions. Bad posture is a big one. Repetitive movements or sustained poor posture are like a pebble in your shoe: at first, it's not a big deal, but over time it can become excruciating.

Chemical stress. These are toxins consumed by mouth, inhaled, or rubbed onto the skin that the body doesn't know what to do with, such as cigarettes, alcohol, medication, pollution, and certain types of beauty products. Whatever the body can't tolerate will cause chemical stress in your system and the nervous system will become overwhelmed. If the nerves that control certain muscles are inundated, then muscle can become unbalanced, causing spasms and, ultimately, spinal fixation.

FEET ARE THE FOUNDATION

Your feet are your foundation. Improper support from your feet limits your progress. If the foundation to a house is crooked, it will forever have problems. With your feet as an unstable foundation, your body will always struggle, and pain in the feet, knees, hips, low back, and your spine will be the result.

There are 3 kinds of feet: 15% of the population have a neutral foot; 80% of the population have a foot that rolls in (pronation); 5% of us have a foot that roles out (supination). The most common form of unhealthy foot biomechanics is over-pronation, when the arches drop, and the ankle rolls inward, causing varying degrees of flat feet. One of the problems we face is that we buy shoes based on look, colour, and price, not on functionality. Buying the right shoes will positively affect the body.

The best way to deal with foot issues is to have an insert/ orthotic, the least expensive being Dr. Scholl's—which will help give a little support for those who do not need a lot. The next level is a speciality store insert which can be found at specialized shoe stores. The ultimate is a foot orthotic designed specifically for you. This will help balance your feet, realign your arches, decrease pressure spots, and, ultimately, allow your posture to improve. You'll feel better, faster—but, like anything else, consistency is needed. You need to wear them often—almost always—to see improvement.

Make sure that your foundation is always supported. It is not great to walk around your house in bare feet on ceramic tiles or hardwood floors; make sure you have a supportive slipper/ sandal. Birkenstocks offer high-quality support. Consider orthotics: They do more than just help correct the pronation.

Next, make sure you have supportive exercise/ running shoes. Always get help from an expert when choosing your athletic shoes.

Think twice about wearing high heels. Although the line of your leg may look longer and sexier in a stiletto, these shoes push the centre of gravity forward, causing the hips and spine to be out of alignment and the back to arch, which will affect posture and potentially leading to lower back pain.

POSTURE

There are many negative side effects to poor posture, besides just looking older.

Without good posture the body can't function efficiently. Think: digestion, breathing, joint and muscle movement, attentiveness, and unexplained tiredness.

A life hunched over computers causes chest muscles to contract, and results in rounded shoulders. As the chest caves in, the head leans forward which, in turn, triggers the mid back to curve and then the spine to compensate.

This increase in workload will cause increased muscle pain and fatigue, such as neck pain, upper back pain, and even headaches and jaw pain. When you are caving forward—such as sitting at a desk, typing, for prolonged spells—you compress your lung cavity. This will affect your breathing and this can affect the functioning of your heart as it is trying to work in a confined space.

When the head is pitched forward there is stress on the lower back. Think of holding a milk jug. When the milk jug is close to you it is easier to hold than if you extend your arm and hold it further away from you.

The loss of normal neck curvature creates tension in the spinal cord, which interferes with the messages sent from your nervous system. The nerves from your neck control autonomic functions such as your heart rate, breathing, and digestion. These are the adjustments my sister received which helped stop her seizures.

To add insult to injury, with women, the more rounded your shoulders, the more your breasts may sag—you can significantly reduce the sag by standing straighter.

Years of bad posture can lead to chronic pain. Have you ever had to help a hunched-over senior trying to reach something on a store's shelf? It's preventable.

So how do you get good posture? Awareness, attention, and work.

Imagine a line from the tip of your ear, down the middle of your shoulder, hip, knee, and ankle. Aligning this way will keep your head over your center of gravity and take the stress off your neck and upper back. If you cannot create this line, obtain chiropractic help and instruction to work toward improved posture.

The same consultation is needed if you find that, on a study of yourself in a mirror, your head is tipped to one side, or you have one shoulder or hip higher than the other.

One of the best exercises to stretch your chest muscles is to put your hands on either side of a door frame and step into the door frame, keeping your head lifted high. This will help open up the chest wall and counteract hours of sitting in front of a computer.

TIPS TO KEEP YOUR SPINE IN BALANCE

When sitting, make sure your chair has low back support. If you are at a computer, make sure that your elbows are at 90°, your hips are at 90°, and your knees are at 90°. This will ease the stress to your system. Get up and stretch frequently—at least every hour. In the car, sit straight with your head an inch or so in front of your headrest. Adjust your mirror to work for you in that position, this will help keep you from slouching as, if you do slouch, you will no longer be able to see out of the back window.

The best way to maintain your posture is to ensure you are always aware of your position while sitting, standing, or sleeping.

BUT WHAT ABOUT THAT CRACKING?

Terrified of chiropractic? Technology abounds.

Chiropractic or spinal health is often misunderstood, even creating fear in some because it is associated with cracking and popping. Technology has advanced. My own practice utilizes a completely safe, non-invasive technique which allows a person's body to be adjusted without any twisting, popping, or cracking.

An incredibly advanced handheld instrument evaluates each of your vertebra for the natural motion of that vertebra. It can isolate exactly where the problem is and, based on the reading of the instrument, adjusts you while you are sitting. It does this by using a high frequency percussive tap that is delivered in a completely comfortable way, so that your body does not tense or resist the action.

EXPECT WELLNESS

- Take some time to understand the mechanics of your body.
- Consider chiropractic checkups are like optical and dental appointments.
- Pay attention to how your body moves: what aches and what feels great.

CALL TO ACTION

VISIT ME ON MY WEBSITE www.drandreae.com

COME SEE ME IN CALGARY.

CALL ME FOR A RECOMMENDATION FOR A CHIROPRACTOR IN YOUR AREA.

HAVING FUN IS THE NEW EXERCISE – THERE'S SOMETHING FOR EVERYONE

"Walking is man's best medicine."
Hippocrates

It's all about the framing. Just as you would select what shape and colour works for that family portrait, or that original painting you purchased, so can you choose the best way to move around. If the word 'exercise' makes you cringe, then say activity, or movement, or having fun.

Fun activities mean more movement. That enjoyment can be solitary and spiritual in walking or running, enjoying the social aspect of a team, family togetherness in games, or incorporating helping—think delivering flyers for a charitable cause. A combination of these work well.

If you enjoy sport, fantastic. If you feel great on a treadmill, and get to watch the past episodes of a favourite show, that's a good thing too. Hopscotch with the kids is exercise. Salsa lessons with your significant other is totally active. Like to window shop? Mall walking is popular. The biggest thing about movement is consistency, and the way to be consistent is to do stuff you enjoy. That is one of the best life-lengtheners available.

Fun activities mean more movement.

Resistance exercise increases muscle mass which increases metabolism, and that means weight loss. It also strengthens bones and helps the heart function more efficiently. People who are active will sleep better, have lower stress levels, and this, in turn, will increase their happiness.

If you choose something involving resistance or weights, then you are on your way to further helping your bones, ligaments, and joints.

I've had first-hand experience with this while teaching in a class where the students, older women, were suffering from osteoporosis. Within months of strength training, women who initially weren't able to exercise or lift weights, due to the debilitating pain of arthritis, were able to regain a level of activity they hadn't seen in a long time.

Then there is the brain. When we're consistently active, we are sharp thinkers, and perform non-physical activities better. Being 'in shape' helps us bring our best to mental tasks. For those who have predispositions to certain diseases, or are in various phases of a chronic illness, physical activity counteracts the progression of such as Parkinson's and Alzheimer's. The more active we are the more independent we will be—and that means into old age.

Adults and seniors who want to stay healthy and independent are advised to participate in four types of exercises:

Strength exercises. Aging naturally reduces muscle mass; this is called sarcopenia. Loss of muscle mass can impact strength, balance, and coordination. Weekly weight training with substantial weight—something heavier than your purse—is hugely beneficial. Think about a backpack on a walk. Consider an inexpensive barbell kept in a hard to ignore spot in your home.

Balance routines. Yoga and tai chi help build leg muscle strength which, in turn, helps prevent falls. The Public Health Agency of Canada reports falls are the leading cause of injury-related hospitalizations among seniors—hospital stays related to falls in seniors are three weeks longer than all other causes. Alarmingly, women fall more than men. If you're not currently a senior, creating an active life now. It will help you when you are.

Stretching. Greater flexibility helps maintain proper posture, helps to reduce discomfort from other activities you're including in your lifestyle, and alleviates issues from sustained inactivity.

Endurance. Walking, swimming, and biking—anything done over sustained periods of time will strengthen the heart and lungs. Start small and build up your endurance gradually. Stroll around the block, do a mall walk, take a short trek along a nature trail, then build up your time, quicken the pace, and add a backpack.

It's never too late to start taking care of your body, even if you are simply adding a little dance to your pre-shower routine, or you're rolling out of bed and stretching while you watch the morning news—or better: viewing an uplifting program. Be sure to check with your doctor before you begin any significant, regimented routine.

EXPECT WELLNESS

- Fun doesn't feel like exercise.
- Evaluate how much time you are sedentary.
- Take note of the differences you feel in your body and mind as you increase your movement.

THE SECOND SIMPLE STEP: EAT WELL

"Let food be thy medicine and medicine be thy food."
Hippocrates

EATING IS ART – ENSURE IT IS ALL HIGH-QUALITY

Picture the brightest colours ever. Emerald greens, deep reds, bright oranges, sunshine yellows. Where might you see them all together? In the produce department or at your local farmer's market. Where else? On your own platter that you have created based on texture and flavour.

If you are the creator of your healthy life—and an artist working on yourself—this is your palette.

We socialize around food; that is a wonderful thing. We can all celebrate participating in cultural practices. However, it's easy to get carried away and eat portions that are too large, and overindulge in sugar-laden products. Then there is the so-called convenience of fast food—a bit of a puzzle since it's just as easy to obtain and eat an apple as it is a super-fish-burger.

Sugar is a major factor in premature aging. It is a culprit in heart disease and diabetes. And it is hidden in many foods. While your blood sugar will rise slightly after every meal, it is not natural for your blood sugar levels to become excessively elevated and stay that way. But if you eat like the average Canadian—88 pounds of sugar a year—your blood sugar will remain elevated.

The processed food industry convinces people, through million-dollar advertising campaigns, to purchase food that will make life easier. It doesn't help that the ingredients are addictive. Sugar—hugely addictive—is a large component of processed food. Add to that, too much animal protein, salt, and saturated fat, and we have a recipe for disaster. Our bodies have been corrupted by additives and therefore have become addicted. With each 'new and improved' or 'low fat' or 'calorie free' brand, there is increased exposure to chemicals—chemicals than can turn on certain genes in our bodies creating the perfect storm for chronic disease.

You live with a lot of rules. You don't need a lot more. Here's a simple way to think about what to eat—it's not the easiest to get used to at first, but it is the least complicated:

Basically, if it's in a can or any 'packaging', and has a list of ingredients which are not recognizable as whole foods, walk away. Processed food is food with a long shelf life—think: preservatives in the form of chemicals, advertised as convenient, usually high in sugar and salt.

> Sugar—hugely addictive—is a large component of processed food.

The British Medical Journal says, 'People who do not eat fresh fruit every day have a 32% greater chance of a fatal stroke and a 24% greater chance of having a fatal heart attack.'

Grandma was right about an apple a day: Swedish researchers found that people who ate an apple a day reduced their risk of kidney cancer by 60% when compared to those that didn't eat an apple.

Most health organizations advise eating five to nine servings of fruits and vegetables every day. Less than half of our population in Canada follow the minimum daily recommendation.

Think about splashing colour all over the painting of you. Brushstrokes of green kale and red beets.

Fresh presents flavour and variety; take a look at how a Mediterranean platter gets the mouth watering.

Healthy eating is not restrictive: It is clever, it is delicious and, once the body is able to understand food addiction/ chemical addiction, and recognize the 'cravings' are in fact no different than needing a chemical fix, healthy eating can restore balance and increase your life expectancy.

If you find that it is challenging and/or impossible to eat like your great-grandparents, then guidance is available. I support a program called Metabolic balance®, an all-natural weight management/nutrition system customized for you. This is not keto or a one size fits all plan—it uses your health history and your blood values, and even takes into consideration the medications you use. It is the most complete program I've ever seen, based on 20 years of clinical research and practical experience. *To find out more go to ca.metabolic-balance.com or www.drandreae.com*

A simple tip is to put a lot of space between yourself and the foods you want to leave in your past. Ordering groceries online is a way to make decisions from a safe place. Even better if you choose a company that only deals in healthy products.

If you do go to the store, you know the drill: don't go there hungry, shop the perimeter. However, you could walk to the store and take a single grocery bag—it's hard to lug heavy cans of prepared foods, flats of pop, and frozen lasagnas. Fresh food is not nearly as heavy. When you have to carry your groceries home, or ride the bus with them, you'll soon discover how many of your past purchases were unnecessary.

ACIDIC AND ALKALINE

Remember in junior high science there were little slips of paper dipped into a liquid to determine if something was acidic or alkaline? Most of us did not take it beyond that point.

Let's go back there. In chemistry, pH stands for the power of hydrogen or the potential for hydrogen. This is a scale used to specify how acidic or basic (alkaline) a water-based solution is. The pH scale goes from 0-14, where 0 is pure acid (some acids burn a hole through steel) and 14 is pure alkaline. 7 is neutral. The pH of our blood is ALWAYS regulated more towards the alkaline side at 7.365, and that will NEVER change.

Our bodies do much better when they don't have to fight acidity. The modern Western diet—processed food—has a massively acidic effect on the body. Such an acidic lifestyle makes it so that there is a constant internal fight to keep its pH level at 7.365.

In 1931, Dr. Otto Warburg won the Nobel Prize for proving that cancer cannot survive in an alkaline environment but thrives in an acidic environment, and his conclusion was that the pH levels in cancer patients are too acidic. That was over eighty years ago, and we still don't get it. Or we do, but we go ahead and, in fact, are quite powerless to fight the 'addictive' powers of processed food.

An easy way to reduce acidity is to drink alkaline water—half your body weight in ounces per day. Adding lemon to your water alkalizes it. Alternatively, you can obtain a system: I recommend Seychelle pure water filtration.

Next, those bright colours for the healthy platter all reduce acidity. Eating an abundance of leafy greens will create positive change in the body. Get them in any way you can (smoothies, steamed, raw). Here are a few of the best:

Spinach isn't for everyone. If you don't like it, maybe it's because it was overcooked. As with all green foods, spinach is rich in chlorophyll, a potent alkalizer and blood builder. It is also high in vitamin K, vitamin A, manganese, folate, magnesium, iron, vitamin C, calcium, potassium, vitamin E, and dietary fiber.

Kale is a leafy green widely known for its ability to lower cholesterol, and detoxify the body—thus helpful for preventing disease. It is extremely high in vitamin K, vitamin A, and vitamin C. Some find it hard to chew, and it is tough. Take a look around in your market and you'll see different varieties of kale. Find one that you like. Blend it in a smoothie, or lightly steam it. Lightly steam means basically expose it to the steamer for only a minute or so (and much less with spinach) until it wilts, otherwise the taste is affected.

Cucumber is a great hydrating food. 95% water, and delicious in salads, smoothies, or on its own. It's a winner.

Celery is in that category as well. Lots of water. One of celery's big benefits is its vitamin C level, and that it contains phthalides—a chemical structure that is known to positively impact cholesterol and blood pressure.

Broccoli, another dark green, is an antioxidant-rich vegetable. Of all the crunchy vegetables, broccoli contains the highest amount of isothiocyanates, a cancer-fighting compound. Isothiocyanates work by turning on cancer-fighting genes. Other vegetables containing isothiocyanate include brussels sprouts, cauliflower, cabbage, arugula, watercress, and horseradish.

Add to your veggies whole grains, clean meats, and nuts.

If you choose to eat meat, clean ones are those animals who were not given hormones, or antibiotics, and were not finished on grains.

Consuming large amounts of carbohydrates leads to a sugar spike in your blood. When this happens, the body goes into overdrive to stabilize sugar levels. This increased spike has been associated with fat deposits. Consuming whole grains—grains that are not processed—especially rye, oats, and barley, creates a slow increase versus a spike. This latter way of eating is much healthier for the body.

Stay clear of foods that have been coated with salt or sugar, or are fried, and have additives. For example, trail mix might evoke thoughts of hiking boots and a mountain path, but chocolate covered candies, sugary cereal o's, and copious commercially dried raisins (coated with preservatives) are not what a healthy hiker needs.

TOSSING IT TOGETHER

Think about the work of art that is you. Curate yourself with colourful, natural foods. Now, think about the visual—the messiness—that would be the canvas of you if you add acid products such as: Donuts, French-fries, potato chips, foods that include hydrogenated fat, trans fat, MSG, artificial sweeteners, corn syrup, processed white flour, breads which are not whole or sprouted grain.

It can get confusing, but even too much of a whole food can become a tipping point. For example, concentrated natural juices are high in natural sugar and are best consumed when diluted with water or, better yet, not at all. Dried fruits are another source of concentrated sugar.

Keep this formula in mind: 70% alkaline foods, 20% moderately acidic foods, 10% acidic foods that can be categorized as an indulgence, albeit dangerous in some cases. If you are of reasonable health, and you are at or near an ideal weight, or you feel that, in order to get to your ideal weight, you want to include those higher acidic foods, then work on keeping them as a once-in-a-while indulgence.

So, how to get so much veg in each day? The answer is a salad a day. The secret to fantastic salads is to ensure lots of ingredients and—here's the key—don't make the same one every day.

Hot salad: Well that's a steamed platter of a variety of vegetables.

Drink your salad? Why not. Have fun, take some leafy greens and some dark berries, and mix yourself a deliciously rich and jewel-toned drink.

REVIEW – FIVE FOR THE WIN

ONE

Eat or drink a salad (hot or cold) a day. Change it up. Use lots of varieties and colours.

TWO

Consume at least 25 grams of fibre every day. A quick check offers up hundreds of combos. If you're eating a good, colourful salad a day, you're well on your way.

Here are a few fibre stats:

Large pear with skin (7 grams)

1 cup fresh raspberries (8 grams)

½ medium avocado (5 grams)

1-ounce almonds (3.5 grams)

½ cup cooked black beans (7.5 grams)

1 cup cooked pearled barley (6 grams)

THREE

Use spices for flavour and for their proven benefits. Turmeric, cinnamon, and ginger are known to have curative properties.

FOUR

Green tea, as it has many benefits to your health including its ability to fight inflammation. If green tea is new to you, please know that a pinch is all that is needed for a large brew.

FIVE

Eat foods high in omega-3 fatty acids as it's been shown to lower the risk of chronic diseases, including cancer, heart disease, and arthritis. This can include eating cold-water fish at least three times a week. A good-quality omega-3 supplement works if you don't like fish or don't eat much fish.

There are your five. Yes, this is a lot to remember. Baby steps. Slow and steady wins the race. Quite simply, if you remember nothing else: eat more fresh fruits and vegetables, whole grains, clean meats, and nuts. Avoid processed foods, sugars/fructose.

WHAT ABOUT SUPPLEMENTS?

Even when we are consuming what is expressed as high-quality food, not all that food has the same nutritional value as it once had—when fields were left to fallow to allow for regeneration of minerals. Nutritional supplements can help maintain and extend your health. Purchase high-quality supplements—that means NOT from big box stores

Slow and steady wins the race.

like Costco, or the popular brands you see advertised during prime-time television. It's like throwing away your money if you buy supplements that do not meet certain standards. I recommend the Metagenics brand to all my patients.

These are the five supplements I take:

Multivitamins: They are essential because current foods are not the same quality as earlier generations consumed. There were fewer pesticides, more local products, and less processed foods.

Omega 3-EFAs: Just about every function in your body, including your digestion, nervous system, hormone levels, immune function, your ability to heal, inflammation levels, and even emotions, are affected by Omega 3-EFAs. They also help memory, cognitive ability, and concentration, and include a defense against cancer.

Vitamin D: Reduced levels are associated with lack of sunshine, and can contribute to the winter blues. It is important for your bones and teeth, and it supports your brain, lungs, nervous system, and cardiovascular health.

Probiotics: There are naturally-occurring bacteria within our gastrointestinal tract. Good bacteria can be affected by unhealthy diets and stress. The effect of an unhealthy diet can disrupt the body's balance of good and bad (bacteria) microorganisms. The GI tract fulfills a critical role in the body's immune system.

Magnesium: Magnesium is involved with over 300 chemical processes in the body. It plays an important role in DNA replication, repair, and RNA synthesis. Insufficient amounts of magnesium reduce your body's ability to repair damaged DNA and can induce chromosomal abnormalities.

Other noteworthy supplements:

Curcumin is the active ingredient in turmeric. It acts both as an immune booster and potent anti-inflammatory. More importantly, it has the most evidence-based literature backing up its anti-cancer claims compared to any other nutrient.

Co-Q10 is also used by every cell in your body. Premature aging is one of the side effects of not having enough CoQ10. It is beneficial to heart health and muscle function; its depletion leads to fatigue, muscle weakness, soreness and even heart failure.

Vitamin C is a powerful vitamin and antioxidant. It helps your body maintain your connective tissue, such as bones, blood vessels, and skin, and is protection against free radicals, which are a source of a variety of cancers. Low levels of vitamin C have been linked with inflammatory conditions.

BEYOND THE FOOD ON THE PLATE—INFLAMMATION

Inflammation is a normal process that occurs if you have an injury or infection. It's natural and you will have experienced it when you've had a cut or infection. The symptoms typically include redness, pain, swelling, loss of movement, and guarding.

When inflammation becomes chronic, it is so low-grade and systemic that often it silently damages tissues. This inflammation can go on for years without being noticed.

Diseases that are known to be triggered by chronic inflammation are heart disease, cancer, and autoimmune diseases.

What causes inflammation? The best answer is it can be the result of a malfunctioning, over-reactive immune system, or it may be due to a problem that you are trying to fight off; one that you are not aware of. Many of these so-called problems are due to... wait for it... an unhealthy lifestyle.

If you are obese or overweight, eat poorly, have a heart condition, do not control diabetes, live a sedentary lifestyle, smoke, have gum disease, or suffer from stress, you are likely suffering from inflammation. At the very least, your diseases and lifestyle are going to create or encourage inflammation.

Do you have any of these symptoms?

1. Frequent headaches and problems with memory and focus, leading to brain fog
2. Bloating and other digestive problems
3. Joint pain
4. Rashes
5. Fatigue
6. Weight gain, even though you are exercising and eating right
7. Allergies
8. Trouble falling or staying asleep
9. Reactions to foods such as cheese, gluten, or soy

The more yeses you answer, the more chance of having or developing chronic inflammation.

If you're eating any of these, you are not helping yourself:

- Sugar
- Saturated fats, trans fats
- Refined carbohydrates
- Gluten

- Dairy
- Artificial ingredients: Aspartame and MSG

You have the power to stop this chronic inflammation and, in so doing, help protect yourself from numerous health problems.

Conventional treatments for inflammation include non-steroidal anti-inflammatory drugs (NSAIDs) or corticosteroids, which can temporarily help decrease your pain, but they are not designed to be taken regularly and do not treat the underlying cause of your inflammation. Medications can make a significant short-term solution, but to begin exercising, eating healthily, and including some natural supplements can help hugely.

There are supplements that will help relieve the symptoms of inflammation while you work at implementing lifestyle changes:

Curcumin/turmeric (as mentioned before)

Boswellia: An herb, has incredible anti-inflammatory ingredients.

Bromelain: An enzyme found in pineapples.

Ginger: An herb offering pain relief and stomach-settling properties.

Resveratrol: A strong antioxidant touted as the modern-day fountain of youth.

EXPECT WELLNESS

- Eat colourful foods.
- Reassign the roles of sugar and processed foods to rare appearances.
- Give your body (and addicted mind) time to get used to your new choices.

CALL TO ACTION

PUT ASIDE A FEW MINUTES TODAY TO GO TO YOUR KITCHEN, LOCATE A PROCESSED FOOD ITEM AND, IF IT HAS MORE THAN 10 INGREDIENTS, TOSS IT OUT.

THE THIRD SIMPLE STEP: THINK WELL

"Health is the greatest of human blessings."
Hippocrates

CLEAR YOUR HEAD, LIVE PEACEFULLY

"I'm so stressed out." "I'm so worried about this that my anxiety is over the top." "I'm scared... what if..." We hear people saying these things all the time. We say them ourselves, too. It's almost as if it is necessary to feel this way in order to sound 'productive'. Many people wear 'busy' as a badge of honour. The busier I say I am, the more important I am. This is completely untrue, but it is what we've become accustomed to believing, and we certainly present ourselves this way quite often. To say we're not busy is like saying we're lazy, right? Wrong.

More work is accomplished, more creativity shows up, and more 'good stuff' overall is achieved when we feel no stress, no anxiety, and no fear—at least not a terror-induced kind of fear (adventuresome fear is great, but then that's more anticipation).

BREATHING BASICS

Breathe from and into your belly. Sit comfortably and, as you breathe, watch your belly expand. You might have to make it do that because many of us don't take very much air in when we breathe. At first, it might seem odd so sit and watch your belly rise and get used to this kind of breathing.

Breathing deeply releases physical tension and increases your oxygen intake—that is a quick way to calm. Adding a sigh to your exhale can also be beneficial, as can picturing goodness going in on the inhale and negativity being purged from your body as you exhale.

It's common to hold your breath when focusing on a task. When you take time out to breathe well, a whole new world of awareness opens up. Slower, deeper, breathing can reduce the heart rate and lower blood pressure. Sleep improves for well-practiced full-breathers. When experiencing pain, breathing is often the key to reducing pain in the moment.

I like to say to my patients: You can't always change the stress in your life, but you can change how you respond to it.

TRY THIS, ANYTIME, TO COMBAT STRESS

Take a little break right now and try this instant stress reducer. Imagine a square in your mind. And the mirror image of it in your belly. Breathe in through your nose for a count of four. Let the air go through your throat into your lungs and swell your belly (while imagining that breath drawing one side of a square). Next, hold your breath for a count of four (while imagining that hold turns the corner and does another side of the square). Now, exhale, through your mouth, for a count of four (and imagine that out-breath drawing the third line on the square in your mind and belly). Finally, wait to inhale again... for four seconds (while you imagine the final part of the square being drawn).

I like to imagine the in-breath is the upline from the bottom up, the first hold is the line along the top, the exhale is the line going downwards to the base, and the final hold being the line along the bottom.

Then, start all over again. Do three or four of these square breaths before resuming your normal breathing pattern.

How did that feel?

DANGER ZONE

Stress is linked to the six leading causes of death, including heart disease, cancer, lung ailments, accidents, cirrhosis of the liver, and suicide. Many medical conditions are caused or exacerbated by stress. Think migraines, ulcers, heartburn, high blood pressure, weight gain, sleep loss.

No wonder people make so many poor decisions. Deciding from a place of stress is surely the way to ruin.

It was a surprise to me to discover that, in the US, the reason for more than 75% of doctor's visits are complaints related to stress . Yes, our neighbours to the south have stats (from the Center for Disease Control) that say 80% of health care dollars are spent on illnesses related to stress.

Remember the fight-or-flight stress response? The one that is made for us to run from predators or fight them. It is a part of our innate system meant to protect and support us. And it did when we had genuine fears like massive animals hunting us. Now, we don't have those physical kinds of fear each day, but we have the equivalent in emotional pressure. And here's the reason why, along with our poor eating habits and sedentary lifestyles, disease is prevalent: we spend way too much time in fight or flight mode. You could say our response can even be stuck in the 'on' position. When we are constantly responding to or operating in stress, our bodies use the sympathetic state of fight or flight. When we are relaxed and calm, we are generally in what is called a parasympathetic state or, more importantly, a healing state.

MEDITATION

Let's make this clear. It is not necessary to sit cross-legged, thumbs to fingertips, candles burning, and chants in the background, in order to meditate. Meditation is a process that can be undertaken in many ways. The description I used above is probably the rarest. Lying in bed, eyes closed, at night, making a gratitude list, is a kind of meditation.

Listening to someone guide you through a kind of check-in with your body, part by part, is meditation.

Many a 'guru' has said that anyone can go to a cave and meditate for six months in an out of the way place, but the secret of true meditation is to be able to sit in Times Square, or some other busy intersection, and still find peace within the self.

OTHER STRESS RELIEVERS

Physical activity, of course. Exercise increases the production of endorphins, your body's natural mood-booster. Even a short burst of exercise can reduce stress. Participating in an activity also distracts you from thinking about things that seem to occupy your thoughts and get you in a knot. And, when you exercise, well, you have to breathe a lot. (When you are on social media, you are likely holding your breath and tightening the body). Movement—all that breathing in and out—delivers a heck of a lot of oxygen to your brain.

Stretching, while not an aerobic type of exercise, can also help stress. With some stretching, including yoga or variations of yoga—think this: put on music, sit in a chair, move your body about. Lie on the floor, move your body about. Slowly and multidirectionally. This helps increase your range of motion, wakes up some spots that haven't been moved multidirectionally in a while, and brings about a focus that is similar to meditation.

Other stress reducers include listening to music, laughing (watch comedy), gratitude journaling, and prayer.

Attitude: Words make a difference. Consider that, when you receive news, a moderated response, versus a reaction, is a gentler way to share your thoughts.

Tribing is a great stress reducer. That means, spending times with friends, and making connections with likeminded people. We are inherently social creatures, so it's no surprise that social activity helps keep us physically and mentally healthy as we age. Social interaction is important in that it has been linked to reduced risk for: Cardiovascular problems, some cancers, osteoporosis, and rheumatoid arthritis. It has also been shown to lower depression and to slow the progress of memory loss.

University of Michigan researchers found that even 10 minutes of daily social interaction can improve cognitive performance! It has been shown that people involved in regular social activities are up to 50% less likely to demonstrate cognitive decline than those who are lonely or isolated.

In addition, those who regularly participate in social activities are more likely to exercise, have healthy eating habits, and engage in intellectual activities such as reading and taking courses. On the other hand, being isolated has been associated with depression, high blood pressure, and a greater risk of death.

It helps to have a plan—that includes daydreaming and then doing stuff to make those dreams come true. A note about that: Evaluate your dreams and discern how you want to feel and what you want to achieve and obtain.

A study at Harvard University in 1979 involved asking graduates if they had written life goals with action plans for their achievement—3% had clearly defined written goals, 13% had unwritten goals, 84% had no goals in any shape or form.

The 1989 follow-up study of those same Harvard students revealed that over a 10-year period the 3% who had written personal goals were 10 times more successful than the other 97 percent who had not.

It has been said that people with clearly written goals which are actively worked on will run circles around geniuses who are unsure about what they really want.

It is a positive step to take the time to decide exactly what you want in every area of your life. While goal is a familiar word, perhaps consider 'standards'. Setting your standards and establishing how you want to feel allows for flexibility on your path—after all, 'they' say the journey is often more interesting than the destination. Fruitful too.

EXPECT WELLNESS

- As you breath in deeply, think about where the breath travels in your body.
- Take time for silence, and customize meditation to work for you—think of it as a necessary and wonderful time-out for reset.
- Consider setting standards based on your core values.

CALL TO ACTION

THINK OF A TROUBLING ISSUE IN YOUR LIFE
NOTE HOW YOUR BODY RESPONDS
TO THE THOUGHT
NOW, DO THE SQUARE BREATHING EXERCISE,
THEN RECHECK
HOW YOU FEEL ABOUT THE ISSUE.

THE FOURTH SIMPLE STEP: SLEEP WELL

"Illness does not to come upon us out of the blue.
They are developed from small daily sins against nature.
When enough sins have accumulated,
illness will suddenly appear."
Hippocrates

SWEET DREAMS

Lullaby and goodnight... oh, if only we had an angelic nanny to sing and rock us to sleep each night.

If you toss and turn most nights, know this: you're not the only one with sleep issues. More than half the adults in Canada report trouble with sleeping, reports the National Commission on Sleep Disorders Research (NCSDR). Not only is there a personal loss within this fact, but it is linked to time off work and productivity, estimated to cost employers $15.9 billion/ year.

The basic recommendation is that seven to nine hours of sleep is required each night. Sure, we have friends who say they can get away with five hours, but that's not enough for the body to heal. The body heals during sleep. We may not be conscious of what happens during that time, but the body is working during that shift—working to heal and restore.

Just as each of the foundational parts of wellness overlap, so it is with sleep and stress. Cortisol and melatonin are hormones that help regulate your natural rhythm of sleep. Cortisol is highest in the morning, which helps to get you going for the day. It gradually diminishes during the day so that your body can wind down to sleep. If you have chronically elevated cortisol due to stress, this can affect your sleep.

Doctors, including Dr. Aric Prather, a research psychologist at the University of California, believe that people who sleep fewer than six hours a night are at risk for more cardiovascular events, more likely to develop diabetes, have increased inflammation, will have a lower libido, and are more likely to have a shorter lifespan. He reports things are much different for people who get seven hours of sleep or more: they enjoy better immune systems, less stress, and lower body weight.

The thing is: When we get enough sleep, our cells are happy.

Let's create the best set up for sleep. Start with the room.

Your bedroom should be more like a sanctuary. It doesn't need to mirror the feel of the other rooms in the house. It's there for sleep and intimacy. That is all. Eliminate clutter, open a window to bring in fresh air—unless it brings too much noise into the room. Keep the room dark. Eliminate anything that creates sound. And I know this is hard, as we are so dependent on our devices, but avoid having any screens in your room. The blue light from your screen mimics sunlight on the UV spectrum—this means it confuses the body. The body, in that confused state, reduces the production of melatonin needed for sleep.

ALL KINDS OF HELP

Side sleepers: Place a pillow between your knees and a pillow that supports your head properly. If you are sleeping on your side, your nose should be lined up with the center of your body; if your pillow is too thick, it'll tip your head up causing stress to your spine, and if your pillow is too thin, it will tilt your head downward also causing stress to your spine. Have someone look at you once you get all set up to ensure you have a proper sleep position.

Back sleepers: Make sure your pillow is supporting you properly by having your ear lined up with your shoulder. Again, if your pillow is too thick, you will tilt your head forward and, if the pillow is too thin, your head will drop back causing stress to your spine.

Stomach sleepers... Noooo. Never, ever sleep on your stomach. It's a quick route to neck problems and upper back issues, and can cause headaches.

Choose a good mattress. How do you know you need one? If you wake up with stiffness and pain that was not there when you went to bed, then you need to consider buying a new mattress. If your mattress feels like a hammock and no longer supports the natural curves in your body, your muscles, joints, and ligaments cannot fully relax at night.

Pillow. Your head weighs 8-12 pounds. A good pillow will support your head, neck, and upper back muscles. My favourite pillow is the Chiroflow water pillow, which helps keep the neck in correct alignment while you sleep.

Time. Go to bed at the same time every night. Yes, even on weekends. It's important to keep your sleep and wake cycle in a regular rhythm.

Naps. If you struggle with sleep at night, limit naps to less than half an hour, always before mid afternoon.

Wind down. That means avoiding vigorous exercise within two hours of bedtime.

Food. Work to have your supper earlier in the evening. If you normally consume alcohol and sugary foods, work to make your evenings free of those foods. Stay away from caffeine, spicy foods, and large portions of any foods once supper is over.

Embrace a ritual so that your brain knows it's time to sleep: A bath or shower before bed, some relaxing music, a chapter in a good book, your gratitude list, a meditation. Your body will thrive with calm ritual.

A good night's sleep starts in the morning. Each morning, open your curtains or blinds—bright light helps regulate your natural cycle. You will hear this called circadian rhythm. Circadian rhythm is a natural, internal process that regulates your 24-hour cycle. In this case, sleep in humans.

Scent. Try essential oils of rose, bergamot, or lavender. Each of these creates calm. If you purchase a high-quality oil, and diffuse it in the bedroom, you'll have another tool to support you in getting a better night's sleep.

Noisy surroundings? Obtain a white sound machine or safe headphones that can cancel noise or play relaxing music

Limit fluids before bedtime. No one needs extra trips to the bathroom in the night.

TROUBLESHOOTING SLEEP ISSUES

There are natural supplements that you can take on a temporary basis to help you sleep better. Magnesium and melatonin are two of these.

If you are still tossing and turning after half an hour, get up slowly, keep the lights dim, and do something boring until you feel sleepy.

One trick, especially if you can't shut down your brain, is to have a pad and pen next to your bed. Write everything that is keeping you awake. This is a powerful brain dump.

We live our lives with such busy-ness during the day that we tend to assign importance to our waking hours. Some of us do that so much that we work into the night in extended career moves, or simply try to get time back that was allocated in the evening to other activities. The day is given this massive 'superior to night' title. This is dangerous. It is essential to your overall health to sleep through the night and rise refreshed. Increased productivity and creativity are happy outcomes of good rest. Imagine being able to make more of a difference in less time when you reassign value to the night.

SHIFT WORKERS

It is essential shift workers take incredibly good care of themselves. If you are a shift worker: please make sure your transitions to and from work are as smooth as possible by maintaining proper boundaries around your sleep and waking hours—be the guardian of your time and make sure your schedule is not disrupted because of the 'norm' of others.

EXPECT WELLNESS

- Transform your bedroom to a sleep sanctuary to create the best place for your body to heal.
- Establish a nightly routine.
- Understand that your sleeping time is not a 'package of time' from which to steal so you can get more done.

CALL TO ACTION

TONIGHT: BEFORE YOU GO TO BED, CHECK YOUR PILLOW TO MAKE SURE IT IS SUPPORTING YOUR NECK AS DESCRIBED IN THIS SECTION.

TOMORROW: PUT THE TIMER ON FOR TEN MINUTES AND DECLUTTER IN THE FIRST STEP TO MAKING YOUR BEDROOM A SLEEP SANCTUARY.

THE FIFTH SIMPLE STEP: AGE WELL

"If we could give every individual the right amount of nourishment and exercise, not too little and not too much, we would have found the safest way to health."
Hippocrates

TOXICITY

We live in a toxic world. We are all exposed to toxins from plastics, household cleaning products, fabric softeners, and we breathe in car exhaust, paint fumes, and air pollution.

The average person uses 9 personal care products daily. Those 9 products contain about 126 chemical ingredients. As your skin is your largest organ, it only takes 26 seconds for them to enter your body. Women are more at risk because we generally use more personal care products than men. 25 % of women apply 15 or more products daily, amounting to an average of 168 chemicals.

Researchers report that one in eight of the 82,000 ingredients used in personal care products are industrial chemicals, including carcinogens, pesticides, reproductive toxins, and hormone disruptors. It's hard to imagine what that is doing to our skin—which is porous, and a pathway to the inside of our bodies.

These everyday chemicals are called endocrine disrupting chemicals, and they interfere with the communication between your hormones and your body. In 2013, the Environmental Working Group identified 12 of the most troublesome hormone wreckers. For more information, please visit their site www.ewg.org. They have a lot of amazing guides to help you navigate this subject.

What is scarier is that it's thought that one out of five cancers may be caused by exposure to these environmental chemicals and, according to a recent study published in the journal Carcinogenesis, this includes chemicals deemed "safe" on their own. Just because they are safe on their own does not mean they're safe in combination with other chemicals.

Without making this a chemistry class, here are some incredibly dangerous chemicals present in our food and personal care products. Avoid these:

1. BHA and BHT

2. Formaldehyde

3. Parabens
4. Petrolatum
5. Sodium Laureth sulphate
6. Triclosan
7. BPA (bisphenol A)
8. PFCs (perfluorinated compounds) and PFOA (perfluorooctanoic acid)
9. Aluminum
10. Mercury

Let's add aspartame here, better known as NutraSweet, which is in a lot of our weight-loss food, and is a known neurotoxin. Neurotoxin means toxic to your nervous system. It is found in most of all gums and candy. If it is sugar-free, it will have some form of it. Look at your labels: If it contains Sorbitol or Acesulfame K, do not place it in your mouth.

This is just the tip of the iceberg. I understand we can't live in a bubble, but the more we remove these toxins from our diets, reduce the use of household chemicals and beauty products, the healthier we will become. Under normal circumstances, your body is able to rid itself of harmful chemicals and pollutants, but the sheer volume of toxins we are exposed to can overwhelm the body's capacity and accumulate in your tissues.

Another list for you—one to promote health:

- reduce use of plastics (stainless steel is a good replacement)
- never heat food in plastic, especially in a microwave
- be aware of EMF (electromagnetic frequency) especially from your cell phone
- avoid stain-resistant carpets and furniture
- use natural cleaners (Norwex, Method, or Aspen)
- purchase natural makeup
- do not smoke, and avoid second-hand smoke
- never consume aspartame, or MSG (Monosodium Glutamate)

I recommend people participate in a detox—once a year is great, every couple of years is good, too. This will help clear the toxins and bring down inflammation. I personally recommend the Clear Change Detox Program from Metagenics to my clients. This 10-day program enhances the body's natural ability to support the detoxification process while providing enough fuel for your daily activities. This is not the 'stop eating' kind of detox program.

In summary: If it's known to be toxic, poisonous, or bad for you in general, then it is probably altering your DNA, which is definitely not helping you remain youthful.

Taking a sidestep: Chronic fatigue syndrome (CFS). Dr. Ray Perrin, a British osteopath whom I have had the pleasure of meeting, has done amazing work on CFS. He has stated that limited spinal mobility, particularly in the middle and upper back, is always present in CFS patients. This lack of mobility can affect the lymphatic system, which is the drainage system secondary to the blood flow in your body. In CFS, if these drainage pathways both in the head and in the spine are not working sufficiently, they can lead to build-up of toxins within the central nervous system.

When that drainage is impaired, it sets up the development of toxic overload in the brain and an overload in the sympathetic nervous system. CFS sufferers have had their sympathetic nervous system placed under severe stress for many years before the onset of the signs and symptoms of the illness. This buildup of stress in the system is caused by: emotional, physical, and/or immunological trauma (think viral infections), and environmental trauma. *Dr. Perrin's website is: theperrintechnique.com or, by all means, don't be shy, I'm happy to connect with you: www.drandreae.com*

TELOMERES

Genes play a role in longevity. Your DNA expression changes depending on your lifestyle and what you are exposed to (it's not your genes that change it's the expression). Many factors cause certain genes to turn on and off. This means what you eat and drink, how you exercise, what you're exposed to, has a huge influence on your DNA, which influences how you age.

Aging is very straightforward: We age because our cells age. The body has trillions of cells that all function together. Inside these cells is the nucleus, which contains chromosomes. These chromosomes are packed with our genes, and genes are made up of our DNA. Telomeres are sections of DNA found at the ends of each of our chromosomes. They are the protective endcap of a chromosome, like the endcaps on shoelaces. Our cells are constantly dividing to repair or replace damaged cells. These telomeres allow cells to divide without losing genes.

The problem that arises with aging is that every time a cell divides, some of your genetic material is lost. This causes the telomeres to shorten throughout your life until your cells cannot divide any further, causing the cell to die. When skin and pigment cells die, we then start to see wrinkles and gray hairs appear. If that isn't bad enough, when our immune cells start to die off, this increases our risk of heart disease, cognitive decline, diabetes, premature death, and a number of age-related issues.

Shorter telomeres have been associated with increased risk of diseases and death. But did you know that the rate of telomere shortening can be either increased or decreased by your lifestyle choices? By making better choices in your diet, reducing stress, stopping smoking, losing weight, exercising more, you can reduce the rate of telomere shortening. This will delay the onset of age-associated diseases, which can then increase your lifespan.

There is also an enzyme called telomerase that can slow, stop, or even reverse the telomere shortening that happens as we age. Telomerase is an enzyme that can elongate chromosomes. Research has shown that exposing human cells to telomerase slows the aging of the cell and allows cells to begin copying again. This is great news. This increase in telomere length is associated with longer cell life, and therefore is key to living a longer, healthier life.

The esteemed professor of medicine, Dr. Dean Ornish, has explained that when we change what we eat, and make other lifestyle changes, our telomeres can lengthen—and our life expectancy is extended. He stated we're not necessarily stuck with 'bad genes'.

Smoking is associated with increased telomere shortening. Research has shown that smoking one pack of cigarettes a day for a period of 40 years is equivalent to taking 7.4 years off your life.

Obesity is also associated with increased oxidative stress. It's shown that telomeres in obese women are significantly shorter than those in lean women of the same age group. This equates to 8.8 years less of life: An effect which seems to be worse than the effect of smoking.

Stress is also associated with increased oxidative stress to our DNA, and accelerated telomere shortening. Research shows that women exposed to daily stress had evidence of reduced telomerase activity and shorter telomeres. This placed them at a risk for early onset of age-related health problems.

If you are not sleeping due to stress, this will also affect your DNA. During your regenerative sleep, telomerase enzyme is hard at work, supporting healthy stem cells.

What we eat can significantly affect our telomeres, health, and longevity. There are studies that have indicated that a diet containing omega-3 fatty acids is associated with a reduced rate of telomere shortening.

Exercise seems to be associated with reduced oxidative stress and elevated telomerase activity and may, therefore, reduce the pace of aging and age-associated diseases. All your choices, good and bad, impact how you age.

IMPORTANT NUMBERS

Let's talk important health numbers. Taking responsibility for your health includes keeping track of your numbers.

Blood pressure

Your blood pressure is the best indicator of how well your heart is functioning. With high blood pressure, your heart is working harder than it should, causing undue wear and tear. This can then increase your risk of heart disease and stroke. Unless you check your blood pressure, you won't know. Taking your bp is easy: most pharmacies have a blood pressure machine. Less than 120/80 mm Hg is a healthy number. 120-139 / 80-89 indicates the necessity to pay attention to your lifestyle and behaviours. 140/90 (or above) is 'high' blood pressure and is a red flag.

In addition to checking in with your doctor, it's important to honestly assess your practices. Add in exercise, lose weight naturally (for example: Metabolic Balance®), increase your omega 3 in fish oil, decrease alcohol consumption, watch your salt intake. It is believed that maintaining a blood pressure of around 115/75 will keep your body performing as though you are eight years younger than your actual age.

Resting Heart Rate

When you are at rest, your heart should be, too. If your heartbeat is fast while you are at rest, this indicates your heart is working harder than it should. This number is tied in closely with high blood pressure. The best time to check your heart rate is when you wake in the morning. A resting heart rate should be about 60 beats per minute.

Waist circumference

The measurement around your waist tells a story. If most of your fat is around your waist rather than at your hips, you're at a higher risk for type 2 diabetes, high blood pressure, and cardiovascular disease. Easily measured, put the tape around your waist at belly button level and breathe out. For women, the healthy number is less than 36 inches; for men, less than 40 inches. Research shows your risk of heart disease increases by 15% with as little as a four-inch increase in waist size.

Body mass index (BMI)

BMI is a comparison of your weight to your height. It indicates how much body fat you have. Being overweight puts a strain on your heart, which increase your risk for things like type 2 diabetes, heart disease, and sleep apnea. To find your BMI go the Canadian site: www.diabetes.ca/managing-my-diabetes/tools---resources/body-mass-index-(bmi)-calculator

Normal weight: BMI is 18.5 to 24.9. Overweight BMI is 25 to 29.9. Obese BMI is 30 or more. However, there are exceptions. For example, if you are extremely fit, then the measurements you take, and the outcome of the calculation, will not be applicable to your health risks.

Blood sugar

Blood sugar levels normally rise after you eat. The danger occurs when your glucose levels get too high, and then remain high over a long period of time, as it can damage your nerves, blood vessels, and your organs. This is way more serious than most people think. Nerve damage in the feet and lower leg is called diabetic neuropathy; it's challenging to treat. This condition is directly correlated to YOUR lifestyle choices. Many patients show up in my office with pain in their lower legs, and feet, and expect a quick fix. This is exceedingly difficult, as you are chemically inducing this condition by ingesting high levels of sugar. Remember our talk about chemical stress?

If you continue to promote that problem in your body, there are adverse effects. You need to know if your blood sugar is high, as then you can take steps to lower it and prevent the onset of Type 2 diabetes, now considered a "lifestyle" disease. It is largely preventable by eating well and getting enough exercise. I believe it is never too late to make a change. If you have diabetes, all these lifestyle changes can help you change the diagnosis.

EXPECT WELLNESS

- Familiarize yourself with the products you use—check the toxins.
- Change out the toxic products you use most often for natural ones.
- Regularly check your numbers.

CALL TO ACTION

IN THE NEXT HOUR: CHECK THE CONTENTS OF YOUR BAG. IS THERE A CHEWING GUM THAT CONTAINS TOXIC CHEMICALS? A HAIRSPRAY? LIP BALM? COUNT HOW MANY ITEMS ARE IN THE DANGER ZONE. DON'T JUST RESOLVE TO CHANGE THEM. VALUE YOURSELF IN THE MOMENT AND DISPOSE OF THEM.

YOU'VE GOT THIS— I'VE GOT YOU

Imagine returning to the beginning of this book and filling in the blanks you might have skipped, or rereading and tweaking what you filled in. Then imagine creating your mission statement—done by knowing what you do (or want to), why you do it (or want to), and how you do it (or are going to do it).

Planning and self-analysis—usually related to personal, family, financial, career, retirement, and health - followed by awareness, are huge stress relievers.

I invite you to think outside the box that many 'self analysis spaces' give us. What if, instead of goals, we establish standards? Like a gold standard.

In Cheryl's example, that is certainly what she was doing. Sure, she could have written lose 10 lbs and run a marathon, but what she did was broader—she set standards based on what she felt was valuable to her. Having a gluten-free lifestyle was created out of love for her son, and so her standard was to have the healthiest lifestyle she could. A goal is often attached to a timeline. A standard is ever-evolving for the better, and is forever.

Either way, goals or standards, the best thing to do is write and sketch out what you want, then do something each day to move toward it.

Another method is to make statements in the present tense. I AM a loving parent. I AM eating healthily. I AM loving my new lifestyle.

To state it in an "I will" keeps it in an unreachable place. I will (one day) be a loving parent. I will (one day) eat healthily. (One day) I will love my life. The "I Am" makes you feel as if it is already achieved.

Each of these foundational elements relies on the others for support. When we exercise regularly, we may not have the appetite for sugar. When we ease off the sugar, we may be in less pain/inflammation and therefore feel less stressed. So, rather than go all in on one category, it's best to do a little from each to get the best effect. And that brings us to how sleep can also reduce stress. Though we may need support to sleep properly, given our lifestyles and the amount of reliance we have on our devices (phones/iPads/tablets), getting a good night's sleep will cut down on the amount of stress hormones flying about in your body.

If stress is responsible for keeping more than 40% of adults awake at night (a US stat), then it would seem like the question is how to get that sleep-in order to reduce the stress. The food, exercise, and meditation will help. Every piece within a strong foundation overlaps and supports the other.

WELCOME THE SAGE

We come full circle to the cover and title of this book.

This is where we tie it all together.

We have lots in common, and we are also unique. Each of us individual. I might operate best with seven hours sleep, you may need nine. I might love tennis, you might like hiking.

The point is, we are individuals and, before we get into specifics of disease and generalities of what we need to be healthy, we need to know ourselves. When we analyze who we are and where we're at—as individuals—then we are in a fantastic place to recognize indicators of how we are responding to our lifestyles and the risks. We can work out what we are already doing that is healthy, and what things we can work on eliminating. We can plan our baby steps to positive change.

If you've enjoyed what you've learned, but feel you need more, there is an online course as an extension of the teachings in this book. You may find that course at www.drandreae.com

Together, we'll move forward to vibrant good health and all the years we put into our lives will be meaningful.

Takeaways:

- Always believe in your significance as a gamechanger and an influencer in the world.
- Get up close and personal with yourself everyday.
- Know where you're at in your life.
- Set YOUR gold standards and employ them.
- Establish boundaries so that your life runs as smooth as possible—without drama.
- Identify what you're already doing to help you live longer.
- Over time, on a regular basis, choose something from this book to incorporate into your daily life, then give that 'something' a chance to take effect before selecting another.
- Revisit the first part of this book, the self-analysis, often.
- Do the grid on a regular basis and with your friends—it's so important to recognize our input no matter how small it seems. Think: Ripple effect.

- Eat, rest, move, and sleep to curate the amazing person that is you—no one else will do this for you.

In a final call to action, please let me know how you are doing. You can comment on my Facebook page or send me an email through my website. I want to know how you are and how I can further help: I'm open to growth, and that means I am open to feedback.

...and... write all over this book, enjoy creating a mission statement, and, above all, EXPECT WELLNESS.

May you experience abundant and vibrant health,

Dr. Andrea

DEEPEST APPRECIATION TO…

My mom, Claudette Holmes,
who took the brave and bold step toward
chiropractic to help her child.
Mom, you made me who I am today. I am forever grateful

My dad, Roy Holmes,
who stood by me no matter my path.
Thank you for that unconditional acceptance.

To my sister, Nina,
No one knew back then that you started me on this journey.

The rest of my family, whose support in invaluable.

A shout out to all my patients over the last twenty years
who showed up, trusted, and healed.

You have each been a guiding light along the way
to writing this book.

True friends are lifesavers, encouragers,
and supports through all the 'times' of life.
These are some of the powerful women who uplift me:

Joanne Neweduk: Authenticity becomes you—you shine,
lead, and have wide shoulders.

Lisa Wolney: You give wise and timely advice.

Michelle Greenhough: You hold me to a higher standard.

Elaine Fawcett: Energy abounds—you tirelessly
helped me refine my ideas.

My editor, Marie Beswick-Arthur:
You 'got' me and showed me my voice.

&

Kudos to Divine Spine's creator Dr. Mangit Gauba, and to
Sarah Richards for the opportunity to fall further
in love with chiropractic.

Spinal
DivineSpine®

DR. ANDREA ESCHENBRENNER

CHIROPRACTOR | AUTHOR | SPEAKER | MENTOR

info@drandreae.com

www.drandreae.com

OTHER BOOKS RECOMMENDED BY BLACK CARD BOOKS

Just Over Broke?
How to Invest in Assets and Eliminate Liabilities
Anna Belov
ISBN: 978-1-77371-133-1

Raising Confident Parents
Secrets from Baby Nurses and Parents about Pregnancy, Infant Care, and Achieving Sweet Dreams
Patricia Porrey, CPD
& Pamela Jones, RN
ISBN: 978-1-77371-073-0

DE PIJN DANS
HHOE GA JE OM MET CHRONISCHE PIJN EN COMMUNICEER JE HELDER MET JOUW ARTS
Caroline Hoogerwerf
ISBN: 978-1-77204-592-5

Tax Tactics For Mere Mortals
Business Finance Secrets That Experts DON'T Want You To Know About!
Ricky Nguyen
ISBN: 978-1-77204-416-4

Sacred Simplicity
Mastering the Art of Knowing the Difference between What You Can Control and What You Must Let Go
Verona Duwarkah
ISBN: 978-1-77204-427-0

IMAGE POWER
Balancing Passion and Profit in Business
David McCammon
ISBN: 978-1-77204-825-4

The Grand Excursion
Stop Camping in the Backyard and Start Enjoying the Real Deal!
Daniel Lantis
ISBN: 978-1-77204-857-5

Minding the Matters of the Mind
A Guide for Anyone Who Has Been Touched by Mental Illness and Wants to Make a Difference
Susan Downs
ISBN: 978-1-77204-878-0

POWERED BY

www.blackcardbooks.com